Crowns of Mercy

Overcoming Depression
with the Word of God

"Praise the Lord, my soul, all my inmost being, praise His holy name. Praise the Lord, my soul, and forget not all his benefits – who forgives all your sins and heals all your diseases, who redeems your life from the pit and crowns you with love and compassion, who satisfies your desires with good things so that your youth is renewed like the eagle's. The Lord works righteousness and justice for all the oppressed."

Psalm 103:1-6

Table of Contents

Introduction

Depression. I don't think there has ever been one word that has taken me to the highest of the highs or to the lowest of the lows than the word depression. If you suffer from depression you know exactly what I mean. That. One. Word. I've allowed that one word to steal dreams, relationships, confidence, life, and sadly, the joy of the Lord. If you're reading this book, chances are you, or someone you love dearly, is suffering from depression. Chances are even better that it has stolen some of the same things, if not all of the same things, from you, too.

Beloved, please hear me when I say that **it does not have to be that way any longer**! Our redeemer, protector, creator, and perfector has given to us a crown more precious than gold. This crown is His grace gift to His daughters. This crown is your rightful inheritance. This crown is a crown of mercy.

The power in the Word of God has authority to break every chain, including the chain of depression. God's Word has the power to transform, renew, restore, and heal. It is living and active. God's Word is a weapon that is given to His children to arm them in defense of the enemy. God's Word is the Sword of the Spirit, and it is sharper than any weapon the enemy has in his possession of which to attack.

Arming yourself with the Sword of the Spirit is the victory Christ has provided to all who believe that He is the Son of God, and choose to follow Him. Beloved, Christ died to set you free from ALL things that keep you, His precious lamb, in bondage. Depression is just one of those many things. Christ came from His heavenly reign, forsaking His crown, to bring to the daughters of God the crowns of mercy. Daughter, straighten your crown, the King is coming!

Section 1:

Hard-Pressed on Every Side

"We Are Hard Pressed on Every Side…"

2 Corinthians 4:8

Hard pressed. On every side. This is what depression feels like, so it's not surprising that the root word for depression means thrown or pressed down. Isn't that how depression makes us feel? Pressed down. Like the sorrow in our soul presses and holds us down without relenting.

Depression is categorized as a mental condition complete with feelings of severe despondency (a state of low spirit caused by loss of hope or courage) and dejection (a sad and depressed state). Depression is much more complex than just feeling sad. Depression is as unique as the individual it is tormenting. Typically depression is accompanied by feelings of inadequacy and guilt, and is often recognized with lack of energy and loss of appetite.

Although everyone's experience with depression is unique, there are multiple symptoms to be on guard for including, but not limited to:

- Depressed mood
- decreased – little interest or pleasure in things
- feeling down or helpless
- trouble sleeping OR too much sleep
- feeling tired and having no energy
- poor appetite OR overeating
- considerable weight change, one way or the other
- feeling bad about yourself
- having extreme guilt
- difficulty concentrating or making decisions
- moving or speaking slowly OR being restless and moving a lot
- thoughts of being better off dead or of hurting yourself

As you can see, depression leads to extremes on both sides of the spectrum. With depression, you can have trouble sleeping OR sleep too much. You can have trouble eating OR eat too much. One minute you may be so tired you can barely move, while the next you are so restless you can't **stop** moving. Depression is a vicious cycle. Like an amusement park ride that is no longer fun, and you're stuck on the track in the ups and downs, on repeat, and the ride has gone haywire. Beloved, it's time to get off the roller coaster. You **<u>can</u>** get off the roller coaster. God's Word can set you free.

One of the promises I cling to is that I can be steady because Christ is steady. As a member of the family of God, I am promised that whatever belongs to Christ, belongs to me. This is my inheritance in the Lord. Because Christ is steady, I too, can be steady. Ephesians 1 is a great chapter to read, study, and meditate on. We are given every spiritual blessing through Jesus Christ. Because of this we have the power to be and have everything that Christ is and has. Christ is steady, so you can be steady.

I'd like to share the remainder of our scripture passage with you. We may be hard pressed on every side, but we are not crushed. We may be perplexed, but we are not driven to despair. We may be persecuted, but we are not abandoned. We may be struck down, but we are not destroyed. (2 Corinthians 4:8-9) The meaning of depression might be hard pressed and pressed down, but when you rearrange the letters in depression you get… **I Pressed On**! Press on my precious sister, your crown of mercy is here!

"The Lord is close to the brokenhearted and saves those crushed in spirit." Psalm 34:18

The Man behind the Mask

When you look at the definition and multiple symptoms of depression, it's easy to recognize the man behind the mask. This "man" presses you down, only to kick you while you are there. He takes delight in it. Although he is always looking for new ways to oppress you, his tactics never change. God's Word says this "man" is always roaming to and fro, seeking someone he may devour. The man behind the mask is the enemy of God. Because we are daughters of the King, he is also **our** enemy.

Depression causes a low spirit because of the loss of hope or courage. The enemy steals our joy so he can devour our hope and courage. The enemy wants to lead us into despair because he wants us to turn our back on God. The enemy whispers, "You're not good enough!"; "I can't believe you did that!"; "You're so stupid!" "You are guilty!" "You'll never be free!" "No one loves you!"; "You'll always be alone!" "You'd be better off if you were dead!" "You'll feel better if you hurt yourself. It will numb the pain." But remember, the only thing the enemy knows how to do is lie. He cannot tell the truth. None of the things the enemy whispers to us are true. Actually, it is the exact opposite. The cross has made you flawless. You are a new creation in Christ. (2 Corinthians 5:17) Jesus has set you free. (Galatians 5:1)

God's Word tells us that our enemy is a thief who comes to steal, kill, and destroy. (John 10:10) He is a thief who takes what does not belong to him so that he may kill and destroy his victim. I spent too many years allowing this thief to steal, kill, and destroy my joy, my dreams, my relationships, and my life. Where there is no vision (or knowledge) the people perish. (Proverbs 29:18) But Jesus has come so that we may have life and have it to the fullest. God gives wisdom, His wisdom, to all who ask for it, generously without finding fault.

God's Word reminds us that we are not unaware of the enemy's tactics. (2 Cor. 2:11) God's Word supplies knowledge so we can understand the enemy's tricks and traps. Because of the Bible, we have a list of the enemy's weapons. Because of the Bible we can stand against the attacks of satan, literally! God's Word is one of the weapons we have as warriors of Christ. God's Word is the Sword of the Spirit.

The Bible is filled with God's written Word, or graphe. The meaning of the written Word is known as the logos. And when you add the written Word + the meaning of the written Word, <u>and speak it out loud,</u> you have the Rhema Word of God. The Rhema Word of God is the Sword of the Spirit. When you speak the Word of God out loud over a specific instance or situation in your life, the Holy Spirit uses the Sword of the Spirit to deliver a death blow to the enemy. Resist the devil and he will flee. (James 4:7)

God's spoken Word brought everything into existence. Genesis 1:3 reminds us that, "God said let there be light, and there was light." The spoken Word of God has power. The same power that rose Jesus from the grave. God's spoken Word has the power within it to do whatever it is that the spoken Word said to do. God's Word never returns void, but it accomplishes What God sent it out to accomplish. (Isaiah 55:11)

Speak the following declarations out loud. They are all true.

I am enough! **I am not guilty for there is no condemnation in Christ** (Romans 8:1). **I am brilliant; I have the mind of Christ** (1 Cor. 2:16). **I have already been set free** (Galatians 5:1). **God loves me so much that He sent His only Son to redeem me** (John 3:16) **because where He is He wants me to be also** (John 14:3). **He wants to be with me. I will never be alone because God promises to never leave me or forsake me, and He will be with me wherever I go.** (Joshua 1:9). **God has good plans and hope for my future**. (Jeremiah 29:11)

Beautifully Broken

God's Word is full of beautifully broken stories of some of the greatest heroes in the Bible who suffered from depression. David was extremely troubled and battled deep despair (Psalm 38:4; 42:11). Elijah was discouraged, weary, and afraid (1 Kings 19:4). Jonah was angry and wanted to run away (Jonah 4:3; 4:9). Job suffered great loss and devastation, as well as physical illness (Job 2:9; 3:11; 3:26; 10:1; 30:15-17). Moses grieved heavily over sin and was filled with anger due to betrayal (Exodus 32:32). Jeremiah was actually known as the Weeping Prophet. He suffered loneliness, defeat, and insecurity (Jer. 20:14; 20:18). And Jesus Himself was a man of suffering and deep anguish (Isaiah 53:3; Mark 14:34-36; Luke 22:44).

These mighty men of God suffered depression, but God still used them to perform miracles, deliver prophecies, deliver people from bondage, and ultimately deliver His people from eternal death. We may be down for the count, but beloved, we are not out! God has plans for us yet!

Although the word depression is only used in the Bible a couple of times, there are many other mentions of words associated with depression.

- down cast
- brokenhearted
- troubled
- miserable
- despairing
- mourning

These words just name a few of the words mentioned in the Bible.

Hidden Treasures and Gems

In my own encounter with overcoming depression with the Word of God, one of the lowest times of despair came to me when I felt God calling me to do something I didn't know if I could do. That brief moment of wonder lead to doubt, fear, and ultimately falling into the enemy's trap, and believing the lies he whispered. I fell into a deep state of despair. Despair that not only affected me, but affected my family as well. God showed me that I was like Jonah, running in fear of what He had called me to do, and God gently reminded me that it is His power that works through our weakness, and that I didn't have to worry about doing it, because He would do it through me. All He needed me to do was go!

When I took myself out of agreement with the enemy and believed wholeheartedly in God's Word, He strengthened and quickened me and almost immediately opened the door for my obedience. Sometimes, God must bring His daughters to the ends of themselves, so His work can be completed in us. Running from God brings despair, sorrow, and grief, but stepping out into obedience, although often times in scary, new ways, brings joy, peace, delight, life, and the crown of mercy.

Be strong and courageous! Do not be afraid!

Section 2:

The Battlefield of the Soul

Battlefield of the Soul

Because we have an enemy who is always attacking, we are constantly on the battlefield. Our struggle is not against flesh and blood, but it is against evil rulers, authorities, powers of darkness, and spiritual forces of evil in the Heavenly realms. Therefore we must put on the armor of God to stand our ground against the enemy. (Ephesians 6:12-13).

The battlefield of our mind starts in our soul. Your soul is your mind, will, and emotions. Your mind is your belief system. Do you believe on and in the Son of God? Your mind is where you believe or not believe. Daughters of the King hear the Word of God and believe. For this reason the enemy's battlefield is your mind, but we have a weapon that protects us; the Sword of the Spirit. God's Word renews our mind. (Romans 12:2)

Your will is your action system. Your will is where you act out your faith (what you believe in). Your will leads to either obedience or disobedience. Daughters of the King <u>desire</u> to be obedient. For this reason the enemy's battlefield will always be our will, but again our weapon is more powerful than the enemy's attacks. God's Word dwells in us and strengthens our will, guiding us to the center of His.

Your love is the perfected work of the cross. Love is the very nature of God. Daughters of the King <u>desire</u> God's perfect love. Perfect love casts out fear and covers a multitude of sin. (John 4:18; 1 Peter 4:8). For this reason the enemy's battlefield will always be in our emotions. God's Word **is** love and there is **no greater love**. God's love is poured out for us and in us and produces the fruit of perfect love. (Romans 5:5).

The Battle Will Rage

When daughters of the King hear the Word of God they believe with their minds, are obedient unto confession, and receive forgiveness of sins through the love of the Son of God. The battle for our spirit has ended. The enemy can never have your spirit. You belong to God. You are sealed by the Holy Spirit, with the promise of God's Word. Nothing can ever pluck you from His hand (John 10:28), but the battle in your soul still rages. If the enemy can't have your spirit, the next best thing is your **joy**!

The joy of the Lord is your strength. (Nehemiah 8:10). For this reason the enemy will always wage war in your soul (mind, will, and emotions) against your joy. If he can steal your joy you are susceptible to all of his attacks, because the joy of the Lord is our strength. Without God's joy as our strength we are subject to doubt (mind), disobedience (will), and every negative emotion. This is why the enemy takes up camp in the battlefield of our souls. He has come to steal, kill, and destroy. Once we are saved he can no longer steal, kill, or destroy our spirit so his next greatest pursuit is to steal our faith by killing and destroying our joy. To understand this we must understand what the joy of the Lord really is.

The Joy of the Lord is My Strength and My Song.

Exodus 15:2

In Nehemiah's time the people heard the Word of God, some for the first time, translated into their own language. Not only was it translated, but it was expounded on by Nehemiah, Ezra, and the Levites who were instructing the people. Immediately upon hearing the Word of God the people felt sorrowful and began to weep and mourn. They had been brought to Godly sorrow, which 2 Corinthians 7:10 tells us leads to repentance. Nehemiah and the other leaders reminded them it was not time for sorrow but a time for celebration! "Then all the people began to eat and drink, send portions, and have a great celebration, because they had understood the words that had been explained to them." Nehemiah 8:12. We receive our strength from rejoicing in the Lord.

Exodus 15:2 says, "The Lord is my strength and my song." Another reason to rejoice! "The Lord is my strength and my song, He has become my salvation. This is my God, and I will praise Him, my father's God, and I will exalt Him. The Lord is a warrior, the Lord is His name." Exodus 15:2-3.

When we look to the other side of the Red Sea, we find another celebration. Rejoicing in God, Moses offered his personal expression of praise. This song, this praise, is declaring who God is, what He has done, and how He reveals Himself to His people. This rejoicing in God is our praise. Our song is our praise. The Lord is my strength and my song. This song is my praise. This rejoicing in God is my garment of praise. Jesus gives us a crown of beauty instead of ashes, the oil of joy instead of mourning, and the garment of praise instead of despair. (Isaiah 61:3) Jesus Himself is our garment of praise.

The Lord is My Strength and My Shield

Psalm 28:7

God is also our warrior and He will fight our battles for us, His Word tells us to just be still. (Exodus 14:14) God's strength helps us to just be still. Peace, be still. (Mark 4:39) God's strength allows His daughters to have peace in the midst of all circumstances. Peace that guards our hearts and minds. Peace that surpasses all understanding. (Philippians 4:7)

As a warrior, God also is and provides the very armor we must wear in order to have victory over the enemy. We must be strong in the Lord and in the power of His might. We must put on the full armor of God, so that we can stand our ground when the enemy attacks. The armor of God consists of the belt of truth, the breastplate of righteousness, the shoes of the Gospel of Peace, the Shield of Faith, the helmet of salvation, and the sword of the Spirit. With our armor securely in place, we can extinguish the flaming arrows of the evil one. (Ephesians 6:10-17)

This next part is just as important as our armor. In verse 18 we are told to pray in the Spirit on all occasions with all kinds of prayers and requests. We are told to not just pray but to pray in the Spirit. We need to pray to receive the Word of God. Praying in the spirit is like the seventh piece of armor. Praying in the Spirit is the unique and vital way we "put on" all the other pieces of the armor. Daughters of the King must be watchful in keeping a diligent prayer life.

The Armor of God

We must wear the helmet of salvation, which is the mind of Christ. We must constantly and continuously renew our minds in the Word of God, who is the very person of Christ Himself. He is our salvation and is the only protection capable of defending our minds from the warfare of the enemy. We **must** have salvation and we **must** live daily in the Word of God.

God has also given us protection for our hearts, the very place where God's Spirit, the Holy Spirit, now resides. God has given us the breastplate of righteousness, as His righteousness, as the armor that protects our hearts. As the dwelling place of the Holy Spirit, the Word of God cultivates the soil of our hearts so that God's Word may take root and grow, producing the righteousness of God in us from the inside out. Proverbs 4:23 tells us to guard our heart above all things, for out of it flows the issues of life.

We must also wear the belt of truth. Truth is the beginning point of all things. Truth stabilizes everything. Truth sets us free! God is the only Perfect One who **cannot lie,** so He is the only source of freedom and stability from the enemy. God's Word is absolute truth and is the very belt that we wear as part of our spiritual armor.

The next item we must put on are our shoes of the Gospel of Peace. Jesus is the Gospel. Jesus is also the Prince of Peace. Only Jesus gives the ability to stand firm in the face of the enemy's onslaught of warfare. Jesus is the very foundation we stand on. Peace does not mean that war is not raging on the outside, but rather that **while** war is raging on the outside, we have stability, calmness, and rest on the inside. The storm will rage, but the Prince of Peace residing in us protects us **as** we wear our shoes of the Gospel of Peace.

Faith is knowing that God's Words are true. Faith is believing that God will do what He promises to do. But the shield of faith requires more than just knowing. It requires action. We must be so moved to action that we "take up" our shield of faith. God is the beginning of faith. He is the upholder of our faith. He is the Author, Perfector, and Finisher of our faith. We must take up the Word of God and stand firm on its truth. For God Himself is the very shield that protects us from the flaming and fiery arrows of the enemy.

The sword of the Spirit belongs to the Holy Spirit. This sword is used in the spiritual realm. It is the Spirit of God who uses this weapon in the Heavenly places to deliver the final death blow to our enemy. This victory is rooted and grounded in God Himself. The battle belongs to God. The sword of the Spirit is the Word of God. The sword of the Spirit is the **spoken** Word of God. When we speak or declare God's Word over a certain or specific situation, the Holy Spirit uses His sword to deliver the final death blow to our enemy. If God's spoken word brought everything into existence, we can be reassured that it has the power to make our enemy flee.

The joy of the Lord is our strength and our song. The joy of the Lord is our strength and our shield. As daughters of the King our eternities are secure, but the enemy will never grow weary of attacking our joy. Be strong in the Lord, in the power of His might, put on your armor, and rejoice in the Lord always! He will fight for you, you need only to be still.

Hidden Treasures and Gems

When Jesus says move, Daughters of the King should move. Doubt is not the opposite of faith. Disobedience is the opposite of faith. I knew that God was calling me to move, to lay everything at His feet, and go, but I lingered far too long. Soon the enemy was attacking me, left and right, up and down. When I woke up and when I went to sleep. There was no longer any peace. The wolves in sheep's clothing had snuck in and caused chaos in the pen. The enemy was being catered to and God's Word was being censored. Envy and jealousy had led to lies, gossip, and accusations. Misery loves company so they found whoever they could to join the game. The very place that was supposed to be my sanctuary had become my condemning place.

I vividly remember driving there, morning after morning, evening after evening, having to build up courage to just enter the door. I had to repeat to myself over and over, again and again, "You are not condemned, Christ has set you free. You are not condemned, Christ has set you free. You are not condemned, Christ has set you free." I had to reassure myself that I wasn't condemned, as the enemy relentlessly caused those around me to offer up their condemnation.

For where you have envy and selfish ambition, there you find disorder and every evil practice. James 3:16

When God says go, we should go. My delayed obedience caused much suffering. I'm so thankful that God uses everything for our good and His glory. Throughout all of the chaos, God showed me blessing and favor that only He can. In that moment, God taught me what it meant to be blessed in persecution. He taught me discernment in recognizing His hand and the enemy's hand, and He taught me how to rest in Him as He fought my battles for me. When I left I was able to go out in joy and be led forth in peace. (Isaiah 55:12)

When Daughters of the King love Jesus with all their hearts, they will be persecuted. But take heart! Jesus blesses persecution. Blessed are those who are persecuted because of righteousness, for theirs is the kingdom of Heaven. Blessed are you when people insult you, persecute you, and falsely say all kinds of evil against you because of Me. Rejoice and be glad, because great is your reward in Heaven; for in the same way they persecuted the prophets before you. Matthew 5:10-12

Daughters of the King will be persecuted because Christ was persecuted, but God blesses persecution. With persecution comes blessing and favor. God's favor. With persecution comes promotion. We grow in God's grace from glory to glory. I have told you these things, so that in me you may have peace. In this world you will have trouble. But take heart! I have overcome the world. (John 16:33)

Section 3:

The Mind of Christ

…take every thought captive…

2 Corinthians 10:5

Depression starts in our minds. Our mind is our faculty of thought and consciousness. Our mind is the invisible world of our thoughts, feelings, attitudes, beliefs, and imaginations. Our minds help us to think, perceive, judge, remember, and speak.

Our thoughts are created by our mind. Our mind tries to help us interpret the world around us. It tries to help us make sense of what is happening around us by interpreting events, sights, sounds, smells, and feelings. Without even realizing it, our minds interpret everything around us and decides if it is good or bad, pleasant or not pleasant, right or wrong, dangerous or safe, and so on. Our minds are constantly giving their own meanings to the events in our life by assigning a specific interpretation to that event. The meaning our minds assign to the event becomes our emotion about that event.

Our upbringing, family values, culture, religious beliefs, and previous experiences make our mind's interpretations unique to us. Our interpretations and evaluations of our events and situations may be very different from someone else's. For example, you may have had a bad experience at a past event, but someone with you had a great time. When you remember the event you may think, "I never want to do that again", while the person who attended the event with you loved it and wants to go again. The event itself was the same for both of you; however, your mind assigned meaning to the event in a far different way than your companion.

The meaning our minds assign to the events we encounter become our thoughts. Our thoughts trigger our feelings. Certain types of thoughts lead to certain types of emotions. For instance, if a certain event seems dangerous or scary, you may think that you are not safe and cannot cope, which leads to the feelings of anxiety or fear. If you perceive in a certain situation that you are being treated unfairly, that may lead to emotions of anger and frustration. Or if the situation your mind has interpreted makes you feel like everything is hopeless, like it will never change, or that nobody likes you, those thoughts can lead to depression.

One of the tactics the enemy loves to us is to make us feel alone and make us feel like nobody likes us. Unfortunately, I have allowed the enemy to make me feel these exact thoughts far too often. These thoughts make us feel inadequate, like we aren't good enough, and often times lead to social anxiety. We must remember that <u>everything</u> the enemy speaks to us is a lie. You have something very valuable inside you. **<u>You are very valuable to God</u>**! Thieves do not break in to empty houses!

As our minds assign emotion to the events we are encountering, our thoughts become automatic. Automatic thoughts can be many things such as words, sounds, images, memories, physical sensations, and sometimes can even be based on "intuition" or a sense of "knowing". Automatic thoughts just happen. They often pop into our minds before we even notice them. We often tend to believe our automatic thoughts, most times without even stopping to consider their validity. No wonder the enemy sets up camp in the battlefield of the mind! Our thoughts are not necessarily true, accurate, or helpful, as they are often based on emotion rather than fact. Our emotion drives our opinion.

Our thoughts can also be quite specific to us. This can be due to past or present experiences, values, culture, upbringing, knowledge, and sometimes for no particular reason at all. Some of our thoughts are so far out of keeping with our "normal" thoughts that we become highly distressed, as our mind tries to add meaning to why we had the thought in the first place. Our mind assigns a feeling to the thought, or why we had the thought, and we think, "I must be a terrible person" which leads to the feelings of guilt and depression.

Our thoughts can also be habitual and persistent, as they seem to repeat over and over, and the more they repeat the more we start believing them as truth. This actually sets off a whole new chain of related thoughts that lead us to feel worse and worse. This is where the enemy loves to keep us. Rehearsing the bad events, our mistakes, and our past failures over and over, again and again, and then setting it on repeat!

Often times our thoughts can be distorted. Remember, automatic thoughts usually pop into our heads without us even noticing it. The following list contains 15 cognitive distortions known to cause faulty thinking.

- Filtering – Focusing solely on the negative and ignoring all the positive
- Overgeneralization – Assuming all experiences and people are the same, based on one negative experience
- Catastrophizing – Assuming the worst case scenario, magnifying the negative and minimizing the positive
- Control Fallacies – Thinking everything that happens to you is either all your fault or not your fault at all
- Blaming – Pointing to others when looking for a cause of any negative event, instead of looking inward
- Emotional reasoning – Believing "If I feel it, it must be true!"
- Global labeling/mislabeling – Generalizing one or two instances into an overall judgement, using exaggerated and emotionally loaded language

- Heaven's Reward Fallacy – Believing that any good act on your part will be repaid or rewarded
- Polarized Thinking – Black and white thinking, not seeing the grey
- Jumping to conclusions – Being convinced of something with little to no evidence to support it
- Personalization – Believing that you are at least partially responsible for every bad thing that happens around you
- Fallacy of Fairness – Being too concerned over whether everything is fair
- Shoulds – Holding tight to your personal rules on how people ought to behave
- Fallacy of Change – Expecting others to change to suit your needs or desires
- Always being right – Believing that it is absolutely unacceptable to be wrong

Because the enemy's battlefield is in our mind, and he does not play by fair rules, God has equipped us with weapons for our defense that are not fleshly, but are spiritually anointed. Our spiritual weapons are not of this world. The weapons we fight with are not weapons of the world, on the contrary, they have divine power to demolish strongholds. (2 Corinthians 10:4) I like the New Living Translation which says these weapons knock down the strongholds of human reasoning and destroy false arguments. These God-given weapons demolish arguments, destroy proud obstacles, tear down speculations, cast down imaginations, and overthrow arrogant reckonings. These strongholds of the mind are used by the enemy to set us up against the knowledge of God, keeping us from knowing God completely. In order to use these weapons we must take every thought captive to make it obedient to Christ. (2 Cor. 2:5) The NLT says, "We capture our rebellious thoughts and teach them to obey Christ." We must teach our thoughts to obey Christ. Jesus Christ is the Word of God. We must align **each** thought with the Word of God. We teach our thoughts to obey Christ by renewing our minds.

...By the Renewing of Your Mind...

Romans 12:2

We are reminded in Romans chapter 12 that we must renew our minds. "Do not be conformed to this age, but be transformed by the renewing of your mind, so that you may discern what is the good, pleasing, and perfect will of God." As daughters of the King, we must not be shaped or fashioned by this age. We must not live after the pattern of a world that opposes God and lies under the control of satan. Instead we must be transformed, or changed in form, by the renewing of our minds. This radical change works from the inside out. A daughter of the King does not think the same as an unbeliever. You are continually renewed in your thinking by the Holy Spirit!

As a daughter of the King, you have been sanctified and set apart. You are transformed, from glory to glory, into the image of Christ. You are transformed in every part of your being, including your mind. When you renew your mind you set your mind on the spirit. God's word says that those who keep their minds fixed on Him, **He** keeps in perfect peace. God keeps your mind at peace as you keep your thoughts fixed on Him! As you renew your mind in Christ, God gives you the power and virtue to overcome.

You have been chosen, called, redeemed, justified, and sanctified. He who has started a good work in you will carry it out to completion in Christ Jesus. God promises to conform your mind into the mind of Christ as you renew your mind in Him. As you read, study, and meditate on God's Word, wear your armor, pray in the Spirit and take every thought captive unto the obedience of Christ, your mind is being renewed. God promises to renew your thinking by the Holy Spirit!

...But We Have the Mind of Christ...

1 Corinthians 2:16

One of the rewards of being a daughter of the King is the gift of our inheritance in Jesus. As joint heirs with Christ, He freely gives us everything He is and everything He has. In Christ we are blessed with every spiritual blessing, including His mind. This is a promise from God, who never breaks His promises. We serve a God who is unable to break His promises. His very nature is truth, thus He cannot do or be something He is not.

God not only promises us the mind of Christ, but His Word actually says that ALL His promises to us are yes and amen! God promises to do what He says. Isaiah 55:11 says that His Word never returns void, but it accomplishes everything He sent His Word to do. There is living power in the Word of God. Power that leads to life. Power that leads to victory. And because this power belongs to Christ, this power also belongs to you.

The mind of Christ is the helmet of Salvation. The Helmet of Salvation is one of the pieces of armor that God gives to His children for their protection. God has already given you everything you need to be set free from the spirit of depression. God has not given you a spirit of fear, but a spirit of power, of love, and of a sound mind. God has given you a spirit of power to strengthen your will, a spirit of love to strengthen your emotions, and a sound mind. God has given you a sound mind! Say it with me…"**I have a sound mind!**" **Yes, my Sister, you do!**

…If You Just Believe…

If you have faith in God and do not doubt, you can tell this mountain to get up and jump into the sea, and it will.

Mark 11:23 CEV

If you believe you will receive whatever you ask for in prayer.

Matthew 21:22

Jesus said to him, "If you can believe, all things are possible to him who believes.

Mark 9:23

Therefore I tell you, whatever you ask for in prayer, believe that you have received it, and it will be yours.

Mark 11:24

Truly I tell you, that the one who believes in me will also do the works that I do. And he will do even greater works than these, because I am going to the Father. Whatever you ask in my name, I will do it so that the Father may be glorified in the Son.

John 14:12-14 CSB

Are you seeing a pattern yet? Do you believe? This is God's Word, not mine! And God's Word is true and never returns void. It accomplishes what God sends it out to accomplish. Do you believe? Do you believe that God will give you whatever you ask for in prayer? Do you believe that all things are possible for believers? Do you believe that whatever you ask in Jesus's name, He will do?

Jesus wants you to ask anything is His name. He wants to give it to you. He wants you to believe you will receive it. He wants you to believe you have already received it. He wants to give you what you ask for because it brings His Father glory. When you believe and receive in faith, and do not doubt, God is highly glorified.

All authority in Heaven and on earth has been given to Christ Jesus. He gives this same authority to His believers. We have authority because Christ has authority, and everything that belongs to Christ belongs to us. Because we are one with Him, we can know what He knows. We not only have the life of Christ, we also have the mind of Christ. When we renew our minds with God's Word and believe in our hearts that He will do what He promises He will do, we are saturated with Christ in our spirit, making us one with Him.

Daughters of the King are reminded in Philippians 2:5-11 that we should have the same mind that is in Christ, who, even though He was God, did not consider Himself equal to God, and came to serve mankind. Christ humbled Himself and was obedient to the Father, wherefore God has made Christ highly exalted, and has given Him the name above every name, that at His name every knee shall bow, and every tongue confess that Jesus Christ is Lord, as this brings God glory. (Philippians 2:9-11) There is power in the name of Jesus, if you just believe!

Hidden Treasures and Gems

I once had a pastor, who hadn't shepherded me for very long, tell me that the reason I was always depressed was because I was always thinking about myself. Although these words were not from God, and they stung, I took them into my heart and began to believe them as true. They festered inside me until I believed that I was just a downright awful Christian, and that God could not use me because I was so self-centered.

God had to remind me that these words, wrapped up in a pretty bow (it was the pastor, after all. Surely he knew God's voice) were disguised as His words, but they were actually from the enemy. Therefore, there is now no condemnation to those who are in Christ Jesus. (Romans 8:1) Satan disguises himself as an angel of light and loves to use God's Words against His children. But please remember, the Holy Spirit **does not** condemn, He gently convicts. Condemnation brings guilt, shame, and death, where conviction brings freedom, life, and peace. Daughters of the King must test the spirits to prove that they are from God. (1 John 4:1)

Daughters of the King must also be very careful with their own words. Proverbs reminds us that from the fruit of our mouth's our stomach is filled. With the harvest of their lips they are satisfied. The tongue has the power of life and death, and those who love it will eat its fruit. Words have the power to speak life or death. Daughters of the King speak life. Your crown of mercy speaks life.

God also, in the same instant, showed me that my depression wasn't caused by thinking too much about myself, but that I had taken my eyes off Jesus. I wasn't looking at myself, but I wasn't focused on Jesus either. When daughters of the King lose focus on Christ, just like Peter, we begin to sink. But just as Jesus took Peter by the hand, He too, took me by the hand and lifted me to walk on water. Jesus is always there to pick us up when we begin to sink. Although they stumble, they will not fall, because the Lord holds them by the hand. Psalm 37:24

The Wisdom of God

…wisdom from God…

Because of God we are in Christ Jesus, who has become the wisdom of God for us, that is, our righteousness, holiness and redemption. (1 Corinthians 1:30) It was God's plan from the very beginning to send His Son as our atoning sacrifice. It is because of this plan that we are in Christ, and Christ is in us. The bible tells us that all of God's plans are good. Jesus Christ in us is the wisdom of God.

In the book of James we are reminded that if any of us lacks wisdom, we can freely ask of God, who gives wisdom generously, to all, without finding fault. God graciously and generously bestows His wisdom on His children as His grace gift to us. This is the mind of Christ. This is the wisdom of God. This is your crown of mercy. Given freely to you, but bought at such a high price, even the very life of our savior. You are loved so much that Christ died to bring you the crown of mercy. My precious sister, please do not ever forget how much you are loved.

Proverbs 1:7 tells us that the fear of the Lord is the beginning of wisdom. God is the starting point and is the very ground in which our wisdom grows. Fearing the Lord is not scary. It is not a fear that makes us afraid. It is a deep love and adoration, so much so that your deepest desire is to please God. The wisdom of God brings favor. Wisdom allows God to pour out His Spirit on us and teach us His words. Wisdom directs our hearts to understanding. It is like finding hidden treasure, discovering the knowledge of God.

Wisdom brings success, integrity, justice, faithfulness, righteousness, delight, discretions, many days, a full life, and well-being. Wisdom brings Christ! Happy is the man who finds wisdom and who acquires understanding, for she is more profitable than silver, and her revenue is better than gold. She is far more precious than jewels; nothing you desire can equal her. Long life is in her right hand; in her left, riches and honor. Her ways are pleasant, and all her paths, peaceful. She is a tree of life to those who embrace her, and those who hold on to her are happy. (Proverbs 3:13-18)

The wisdom from above is pure first of all; it is also peaceful, gentle, and friendly; it is full of compassion and produces a harvest of good deeds; it is free from prejudice and hypocrisy. And goodness is the harvest that is produced from the seeds the peacemakers plant in peace. (James 3:17-18 Good News Translation)

When we allow the Holy Spirit to produce the fruit of wisdom in us, we are offered the promised rewards of a full life and well-being (peace and wholeness) which often manifests in us as a healthy lifestyle and freedom from anxiety. Righteous living tends to offer a happier and healthier life. Jesus is our righteousness. The bible says that we all have sin, and we all fall short of the glory of God, but Jesus has come to replace our dirty rags with the white robe of His righteousness, all because He loves us. You, my precious sister, are dearly loved!

Wisdom is to be deeply desired and praised. God Himself possess wisdom, created the world by wisdom, and governs the world by wisdom. The same wisdom God used to create our world is the same wisdom God gives us, so that we can successfully live in the world He created. Wisdom is His grace gift to us, and He is ready and able to give, when we are ready to receive. Ask and you shall receive. Until now you have not asked for anything in my name. Ask and you will receive, and your joy will be made complete. (John 16:24)

Crowns of Mercy

When we strip everything away, only the perfect love of God remains. God's love covers a multitude of sin. God's perfect love casts out fear. God's perfect love is your crown of mercy. Your crown because you are a daughter of the King.

I am true vine, and my Father is the gardener. He cuts off every branch in me that bears no fruit, while every branch that does bear fruit He prunes so that it will be even more fruitful. You are already clean because of the word I have spoken to you. Remain in me, as I also remain in you. No branch can bear fruit by itself, it must remain in the vine. Neither can you bear fruit unless you remain in me. I am the vine; you are the branches. If you remain in me and I in you, you will bear much fruit; apart from me you can do nothing. If you do not remain in me, you are like a branch that is thrown away and withers; such branches are picked up, thrown into the fire and burned. If you remain in me and my words remain in you, ask whatever you wish, and it will be done for you. This is to my Father's glory, that you bear much fruit, showing yourselves to be my disciples. As the Father loved me, so have I loved you. Now remain in my love. If you keep my commands, you will remain in my love, just as I have kept my Father's commands and remain in His love. I have told you these things so that my joy may be in you and that your joy may be complete. My command is this: Love each other as I have loved you. Greater love has no one than this: to lay down one's life for one's friends. You are my friends if you do what I command. John 15:1-14

Jesus came from the throne of His Kingly reign, to the earth that He created, to exchange His live to give you a crown. You will receive a crown of life in Heaven, but Jesus also died to give you a crown here on earth.

Jesus died to give you the crown of mercy. Whenever you feel overwhelmed, remember whose daughter you are, and straighten your crown.

Other Books by the Author

Tea for Two: A Mother& Daughter Tea Party Bible Study

Available on Amazon in eBook and paperback

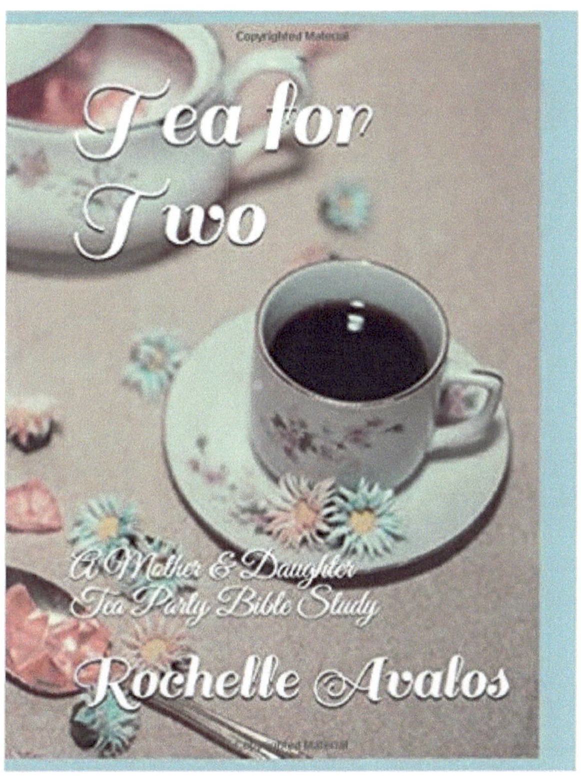

You are cordially invited to a Mother& Daughter tea party Bible study hosted by your Maker! A delightful and engaging encounter into God's Word for mothers and daughters of all ages. A tea party fit for God's princess! Journey together through God's Word to find out how God says we are like tea cups, all while enjoying a tea party with your princess. Complete with journaling pages, activities, crafts, and vivid images. May your cup always run over!

Fishers of Men:

A Guide to Becoming Disciples of Christ and Fishers of Men

Available on Amazon in paperbook and eBook

Join us as we embark on a journey becoming Disciples of Christ and fishers of men. With Jesus as our Master Teacher, learn how disciples are chosen and called, and what we need to do when responding to that call, and the amazing rewards and blessings for those who choose to follow. This guide will have three features; a bible study, the Catch of the Day, and a section for Casting Thoughts. The Bible study is designed as a daily devotional; however, you may decide to complete each new chapter with the first devotion of each week. Or you can space them out, it's entirely up to you! The Catch of the Day contains extra "nuggets" of scripture, messages, information, and encouragement. Casting Thoughts is at the end of each chapter and provides designated days for reading and journaling through the four Gospels. We pray that this guide helps you in becoming Disciples of Christ and fishers of men and empowers you to go and make disciples!